Teaching
Ancient Greece

John Fines

Jon Nichol

Ray Verrier

Edited by Jacqui Dean

First published in Great Britain by Heinemann Educational Publishers
Halley Court, Jordan Hill, Oxford OX2 8EJ
a division of Reed Educational and Professional Publishing Ltd

MELBOURNE AUCKLAND FLORENCE PRAGUE MADRID ATHENS
SINGAPORE TOKYO SAO PAULO CHICAGO PORTSMOUTH NH MEXICO
IBADAN GABORONE JOHANNESBURG KAMPALA NAIROBI

Typeset by Gecko Limited
Printed by Athenæum Press Ltd, Gateshead, Tyne & Wear
Illustrations by Jane Bottomley and Mike Parsons

00 99 98 97
10 9 8 7 6 5 4 3 2 1

ISBN 0 435 32173 0

Cataloguing in Publication Data is available from the British Library

Acknowledgements
The Publishers would like to thank the following for permission to reproduce
photographs: Chris Honeywell, cover, p.18; Ronald Sheridan/Ancient Art and
Architecture Collection, pp.14, 46, 48.

The cover masks are reproduced courtesy of Sarah and Matthew Purrsell

Our special thanks to the headteachers, staff and children at Midhurst
Intermediate School, Midhurst, West Sussex; South Bersted Primary School,
Bognor Regis, West Sussex; and Landscore Primary School, Crediton, Devon.

The Personal Voice: Throughout this book, members of the Nuffield Primary
History Team have used the personal voice when describing their part in lessons
and lesson planning. The three different individuals involved have decided not to
separately identify themselves, but to be a personal, but anonymous 'I' in this
context.

Every effort has been made to contact copyright holders of any material
reproduced in this book. Any omissions will be rectified in subsequent printings if
notice is given to the Publisher.

Contents

List of Illustrations

The Nuffield Primary History Project

In 1991 the Nuffield Foundation gave its support to a new primary history project which aimed to examine the National Curriculum and explore its implications for the teaching of primary history. During the past five years John Fines, Jon Nichol, Jacqui Dean and Ray Verrier have worked alongside classroom teachers in a wide range of schools, experiencing the reality of primary history teaching and learning.

What we did was to teach the full range of the National Curriculum in history, at least twice, and, in some cases, four times. We did this in a wide variety of settings, from tiny country schools with a total enrolment of 43, to huge triple deckers in London; from schools in the urban North, to schools in the suburban South. We taught good children and wild children, clever children and those called special – we tried the lot.

Part of our aim was to provide narratives of these varied experiences. We felt that at this time of great change, the last thing teachers needed was theoretical statements about how things might happen. What we could best do would be to say, quite simply, here is what happened to *us* teaching the Greeks. It might give you a laugh and stimulate you to think just how *you* want to do it. We list our resources in case you want to take on board any of our practical ideas, and we give examples of children's work so that you can see some comparisons with the children in your own class. In this, as in all things, we have tried to be scrupulously honest, and have not edited the children's work at all, except for corrected spelling.

NPHP's five principles

Throughout, the Project's work has been based on 'doing history', as encapsulated in the five principles below:

1 **Questioning** History is about asking and answering questions, and, above all, getting children to ask questions.
2 **Challenges** In both our materials and in the questions we ask of children, we challenge them to persist, to speculate, to make connections, to debate issues, to understand the past from the inside.
3 **Integrity and economy of sources** We teach real history, so that what we use are authentic sources of history. More wide-ranging and useful questions can be asked of a few well chosen sources than from an unfocused jumble.

4 **Depth** Real historical knowledge, even at primary level, demands study in depth. Only by getting deeply inside the past can pupils develop expertise and confidence.

5 **Accessibility** We make history accessible to all children by starting with what the children can do and building on that. This is done by using a wide variety of teaching approaches, including well paced whole-class teaching, co-operative pair work and group work.

At the heart of the curriculum

A good part of the business of teaching history is to recognize the place of history at the heart of the curriculum. History is interesting and there is a lot of it, enough so that at all stages, and in all other parts of the curriculum, learning can take place via history. It doesn't need to be thought of as an item contending with all the subjects in an over-full curriculum – history using the right approach can be the real heart of it all, the centre of the wheel from which all of the spokes radiate.

Introduction

Many teachers find the Ancient Greece Study Unit more than a little daunting. This is not surprising, for the pre-1995 History National Curriculum specified no less than seven areas of study ranging from the Bronze Age period to Greece and Rome, taking in en route the economy, everyday life, the city state, the arts and the Persian Wars. True, the current orders have reduced this massive coverage to five areas of study. But, the topics still range over a period of almost 2,000 years, and require study in detail of subjects that have exercised the best academic minds for centuries.

The Ancient Greece History Study Unit

'Pupils should be taught about the way of life, beliefs and achievements of the ancient Greeks and the legacy of Ancient Greek civilization to the modern world:

The Ancient Greeks

a Athens and Sparta – e.g., *everyday life, citizens and slaves.*

b arts and architecture – e.g., *pottery, sculpture, theatres, temples, public buildings, and how these help us to find out about the Ancient Greeks.*

c myths and legends of Greek Gods and Goddesses, heroes and heroines.

d relations with other peoples – e.g., *Persians with stories of Marathon, Thermopylae and Salamis, the Greeks in southern Italy, the campaigns of Alexander the Great, the influence on the Greeks of other civilizations, such as Egypt or Rome.*

The legacy of Ancient Greek civilization

e influence on the modern world – e.g., *politics, language, sport, architecture, science.*'

Problems teaching the Ancient Greece Study Unit

A major difficulty for most primary teachers is that few of them have studied Ancient Greece at school or college. Thus the programme of study looks strange and unfamiliar and even after absorbing new information, the teacher still faces the task of constructing a teaching scheme, finding suitable resources and planning and delivering lessons.

Planning and teaching the HSU

It is the NPHP aim to offer teachers help, assistance and advice in planning and teaching **Ancient Greece** at Key Stage 2. Over the past four years the Project has been working in schools on all the History Study Units. We have taught the **Ancient Greece** Study Unit on four occasions. This book takes readers into three of these schools to show contrasting ways of approaching this HSU.

The three teaching accounts	The three examples covered were taught in very different schools, with age groups from Years 5 and 6. In each school the teaching programme was planned and taught to fit the history scheme of work operating in the school concerned.
The three examples and the interrelation of ideas and strategies	The examples are not blueprints for action as every class is different and what might suit one class may not suit another. However, they all illustrate what we mean by 'doing history' with children. It is our hope that teachers preparing to teach the Ancient Greece HSU will find underlying perceptions, strategies, teaching and learning ideas and suggestions that they can adapt to their circumstances. We hope that in some of our lessons, and indeed whole topics, the teaching strategies or resources suggested will strike a chord with teachers, and that they will find inspiration and useful material to adapt for their own classes.
The narrative style	We have used a narrative style to report the teaching, as this seems to give the most realistic account of what happened. Each account starts with a brief outline of the project and a description of the school context in which we worked. The teaching is therefore sign-posted so that a reader can rapidly form a mental map of the entire project and then, if desired, turn to a particular lesson that is of interest. Alternatively the reader may wish to start with a straight reading of the entire teaching to obtain a feel for the pace and development of the topic and how its elements interrelate.
	Throughout we have included examples of children's work – covering written, pictorial and oral responses as well as contributions to discussion sessions. We also have noted the major resources used in each topic to illustrate or support the teaching.
Extension of teaching ideas and strategies	In the NPHP companion volume, *Teaching Primary History* (Heinemann, 1997), we give a detailed explanation of individual teaching techniques. So, for example, a teacher interested in finding out how to incorporate storytelling or drama into his or her repertoire can learn how to develop and apply that teaching strategy using the vast range of exemplar material in *Teaching Primary History*.

Ancient Greece at South Bersted Primary School
Introduction

The two Year 5 and Year 6 classes at South Bersted had already covered a number of topics in the Ancient Greece HSU. Our planning involved the single new topic of buildings, but also covered myths and legends. The teaching was planned around Key Element 3 of the History National Curriculum (Interpretations of History) using the varying interpretations of archaeologists to explain the purpose of the palace of King Minos at Knossos in Crete. A visit at the end of the project to Fishbourne Roman Palace was planned to give pupils the opportunity of working as archaeologists on a real historical site. The question the pupils worked on was 'Did Evans get it right? Was it really a palace building?'

The decision to focus on the Palace at Knossos was made for several reasons:

- Varying interpretations of this building would provide a good basis for developing Key Element 3.
- The pupils could adopt the role of archaeologists and thereby discover something about the working methods of archaeologists and the ways in which they interpret the past. The visit to Fishbourne Roman Palace would give the pupils a chance to use some of the archaeological and research skills acquired during the work on Knossos. In addition, the buildings at Knossos and Fishbourne are both presented to visitors as palaces.

Planning

After discussion with the teachers our teaching plan developed as follows:

Session 1 A story told by me about Arthur Evans at school hearing from his history teacher the story of Theseus and the Minotaur.

Session 2 Practical workshop based on pupils using a box of Roman artefacts on loan from Chichester District Museum.

Session 3 Pupils to make their own plan of what they think a palace might look like.

Session 4 Pupils examine Arthur Evans' plan of his findings at Knossos and decide how the different rooms and spaces might be identified in the context of a palace building.

Session 5 Pupils examine pictures of some of the objects found at Knossos. What do these objects suggest about the possible function of the building?

This would be followed by the visit to Fishbourne Roman Palace for the pupils to exercise their skills as archaeologists in a new context.

Resources

There are a number of books which give teachers some background knowledge and resources for the Palace of Knossos. The ones I found particularly useful were:

R Burrell and P Connolly, *The Greeks*, OUP, 1989.

Aileen Plummer, *People and Pictures, Studies in Empathy*. Holmes McDougall, 1984 (see Chapter 4, 'The Search for Minos and the Minotaur').

James Mason, *Ancient Greece Resource Book*. Longman, 1991.

Rodney Castleden, *The Knossos Labyrinth, A New View of the Palace of Minos at Knossos*. Routledge, 1990.

The first three listed are suitable for use by pupils, but the last is an academic book which offers a substantial background to a number of interpretations of the palace building, as well as containing many excellent photographs.

The teaching pattern

I worked with two classes separately, but covered the same teaching programme, half a morning with each class.

Session 1 Theseus and the Minotaur

The pupils had already covered a number of topics of the Ancient Greece HSU, including Greek myths and the location and geography of Greece.

Learning objectives

This first session focuses on the question of story evidence and its interpretation, using the story of Theseus and the Minotaur.

The teaching

Asking questions: pooling ideas

I began by asking the class how we know about people who lived as long ago as the Ancient Greeks. Quickly the pupils came up with the word 'archaeologist' and I pooled their various ideas about the meaning of this term on the board.

Arthur Evans: the archaeologist and the story of the Minotaur

Next I introduced the name of a famous archaeologist, Arthur Evans, and said that when he was a schoolboy he heard his teacher tell the story of Theseus and the Minotaur. I was going to tell them this story, which we call a myth. But, before telling the class the story, I asked them to explain what they thought a myth was. We discussed their ideas about a myth containing some elements that were probably true and others that were not.

Using the story as evidence

After I finished the story we began thinking about the content. The pupils jotted down, with reasons, aspects that they considered:

- definitely true
- may have been true
- definitely not true

Class discussion: sharing ideas

We then discussed as a class what the children thought about the story. Some very interesting ideas emerged on what may have been true, or not true, with marked differences of opinion and varying interpretations of the Minotaur, such as a man-eating bull, or a badly formed bull. In offering reasons many pupils drew upon their own ideas of what seemed reasonable, for example the view that normal parents simply would not let their children be sent off to the Minotaur.

Here are some examples of the pupils' reasoning, based on their interpretation of the story:

Not true that the Minotaur existed because:
impossible for it to exist
don't believe in that creature
feeding it would be difficult
could not live in those conditions
people would not send children to be taken by the Minotaur
parents would protect their children.

May be true that the Minotaur existed because:
a man-eating bull as a description could have existed
could have been a badly deformed bull.

Definitely true that Aegeus threw himself into the sea because:
the Aegean Sea was named after him and the Aegean Sea exists, checked by pupils on a map.

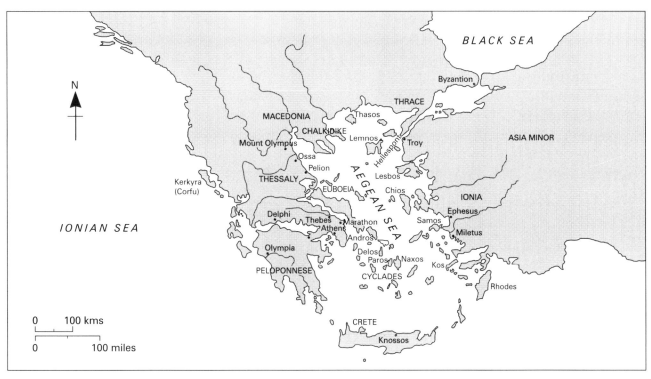

Illustration 1: *A map of Ancient Greece*

Handling artefacts is an exciting way of directly involving children with people from the past. Although having a local museum with a good loan service is enormously valuable, there are alternative sources, such as shops which sell historical reproductions, some by mail order. Roman artefacts, which can be borrowed from many museums, provided a good substitute for Greek objects, which are far more difficult to have on loan for classroom use. Fortunately we were able to borrow a box of artefacts for half a term so that the pupils could examine these objects over a period of time. However, this exercise could be done using other historical objects which teachers could gather for themselves. Alternatively postcards and pictures of Greek artefacts can be used.

Learning objectives

My intentions in this session were to give each class an opportunity of handling and discussing objects from the past and, through this experience, to develop a preliminary understanding of some aspects of how an archaeologist works and the nature of archaeological evidence.

Resources

The resources used in this session were part of a light bulb, part of a bicycle, the arm rest of a student chair, Roman objects and an Archaeologist's report sheet (see Illustration 2).

The teaching

Investigating modern objects: known to unknown

As the children had little prior experience of working with objects, I started the session with a number of modern fragments: part of a bulb, part of a bicycle and the arm rest of a student chair.

Questions: putting children into the shoes of people in the past

I then put to the class this question which we discussed as a class: *'Imagine we are living 300 years in the future and discover these objects used by people living in the 1990s. What would we make of them?'*
This proved a useful starting point which generated varied ideas.

Investigating Roman objects

Next the pupils divided into groups to examine ten Roman objects loaned from the Chichester District Museum (a question sheet was also included). The Roman box contained a bronze brooch, coins, a fragment of wall plaster, a bronze decorated pin, a cooking platter, a cooking pot and a replica lamp.

Working in groups, observation and recording

The class was given about half an hour to examine, in groups, one of the Roman artefacts and to record their observations on the Archaeologist's report sheet. Each group finally reported back their ideas to the class.

Name..

Drawing of the object

What colour(s) is it? _____

What is it made of?_____

Is the object complete or is it a fragment? _____

Is the object handmade or machine-made? _____

How do you know? _____

What do you think the object was used for? _____

_____

Is the object decorated or just plain? _____

Measure the object and write down:

its height or length_____

its width_____

How heavy is it?_____

Has the object any writing of any sort? _____

What does it say? _____

_____

Do we have any objects like this today?_____

Draw a modern object like it overleaf

Illustration 2: *An archaeologist's report sheet*

Group discussion	The range of discussion which actually took place is not fully reflected in the written responses. For example, a group of girls examining the replica bronze oil lamp spent some time working on the idea of its being used for medicine water, having decided that their original idea of a water or wine container would not really work. They tested out this first idea with water and then decided on a container for a small quantity of liquid for a special purpose, such as medicine. They later changed their ideas to a small musical instrument, and, finally, decided it was an oil lamp. In making an assessment of this activity it is necessary to take account of the oral work and not only the final written responses.

Session 3 — Knossos: thinking about palaces

We now moved on to the topic of Ancient Greek buildings, with a study of the Minoan palace of Knossos in Crete. Palaces are amazingly complex structures that reflect their social, political, legal and economic functions. How can we help children to make sense of them? The lesson began by giving pupils the task of creating a palace. We were in effect encouraging the children to imagine an old, large palace building in terms of spaces and their size, layout and function. We also thought back to the Theseus story and recalled the labyrinth – for if the Knossos palace was indeed the location for the Theseus story, we might expect to find evidence of the labyrinth.

Learning objectives	The learning objectives for this session were to help children to understand the nature of old palace buildings and to relate this understanding to a possible interpretation of the story of Theseus and the Minotaur in relationship to the plan of the building at Knossos.
Resources	I used the Castleden book on Knossos and provided each pupil with a large sheet of paper.

The teaching

Review of Arthur Evans	I started the session by recalling the name of Arthur Evans introduced, briefly, in Session 1.
The story of Evans and Knossos	I decided to tell the children, in a story form, how Evans became interested in archaeology and how this interest led to his dig at Knossos in 1900. I obtained the information about Evans from Castleden's book. I then turned this into a story, using the strategies developed in the NPHP companion volume, *Teaching Primary History* (Heinemann, 1997).

The outline of the story is as follows:

- Evans' family and home life as a child
- His interest in small objects
- His early travels to the Balkans and Turkey
- His job as special correspondent to the *Manchester Guardian*
- Reconstruction of Evans' meeting with Heinrich Schliemann
- Evans' finding of the three and four sided stones in the antique dealers' trays in Athens
- His meeting with Minos Kalokairinos
- His problems gaining access to the excavation site
- Start of excavation in 1900
- The discovery of the Throne Room.

These are the building blocks for the story I told the children. But, as the teacher, I had to convert these dry 'basic facts' into the colour and excitement of what was a truly fascinating story.

I deliberately finished my story at the point where Evans unearthed what he considered to be the Throne Room of the 'Palace' of King Minos. He was starting to put his interpretation on the site – it was now part of a palace complex.

A question

After telling the story up to the point of the Throne Room discovery I asked the children the following question:
'If you were an archaeologist, and thought that you had found the remains of a palace, what type of 'spaces' would you be looking for? What would the rooms, courtyards and area around the palace be used for?'

Children's responses

On the board I built up the children's ideas of the type of rooms and spaces they associated with a palace building. After a considerable time spent discussing ideas I gave each pupil a large sheet of paper and asked them to prepare a plan of a palace-type building showing the sort of room spaces Arthur Evans might hope to excavate if his interpretation of what a palace might be like was true. The children worked for about half an hour on their plans, discussing and exchanging ideas, but each pupil was required to present his or her own plan.

Analysis of the pupils' plans

Once again I took away the children's work and in looking through the plans I was especially interested in two aspects:

1 **Arranging spaces** Were the pupils simply arranging rooms in random order or was there any attempt to group them according to some sort of logic? For example, did the arrangements show a range of related rooms to serve the domestic needs of the royal family?

2 **Logical thinking** Were any attempts made to introduce a logic to the entire building? For example, was the palace built around a focal point?

Both aspects were untutored, as I did not give the pupils any hints beforehand on how to arrange the palace. The second point seemed particularly important in so far as the Palace of Knossos appears as a rather confused jumble of rooms showing nothing of the balance and symmetry of classical Greek buildings.

The result of my examination of the children's work in terms of my first point showed up a sense of logic in their arrangements of the room layout, for example, store room and dining area were related; a waiting room was next to a small throne room; the king's and queen's bedrooms and dressing rooms were related areas; the kitchen, dining room and food stock rooms were in related areas; money, treasury and counting rooms were related and stables, chariot and horse training areas were grouped together.

Two pupils considered features not included by other children:

- window spaces marked out on the plan
- a plan showing location of locks and keys to all rooms.

In terms of the second point (a logic to the entire building) some interesting designs emerged, such as making a throne room the focal point of the palace, a plan in which a series of wedge-shaped rooms all pointed towards the labyrinth, a plan showing a variety of room shapes linked by many maze-like passages, a plan making the throne room the focal feature from which radiated maze-like winding passages, a design which included a long hall running the entire length of the building, ending at the throne room and a plan showing a winding set of passageways.

Session 4 Using Arthur Evans' plan of the Palace of Minos at Knossos

During this session we were going to try to make sense of Arthur Evans' ground plan of the Palace of Minos at Knossos. Considerable time was devoted to a class discussion in which we explored the pupils' ideas on the possible function of this unusual building plan if it were not a palace as Evans thought.

Learning objective

The learning objective for this session was to make sense of the plan of the Palace of Minos at Knossos, as drawn up by Arthur Evans.

Resources

The resource used for this session was a copy of the plan of the Palace of Minos (Illustration 3)

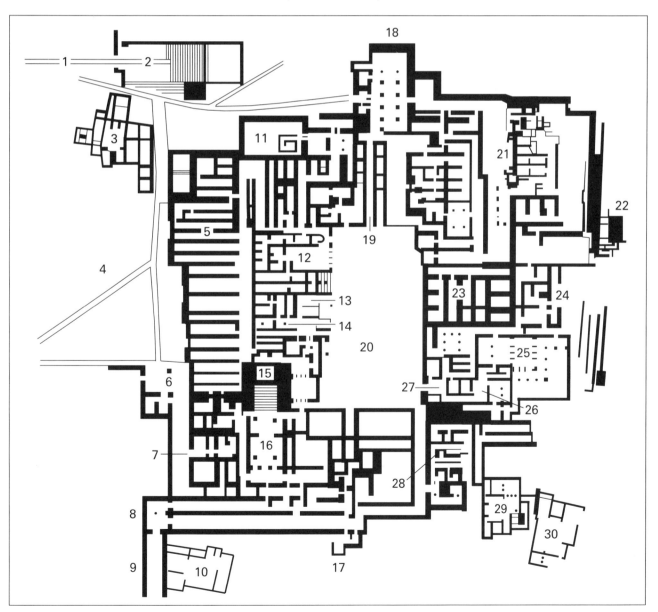

Illustration 3: *A plan of the Palace of Minos at Knossos*

The teaching

Comparisons

I began this session by getting the pupils to compare and contrast their own plans for a palace-type building. How were the plans similar? How were they different? This gave the classes an opportunity to remember the previous week's work, as well as preparing them to look at Evans' plan of Knossos.

The Knossos plan

I gave each pupil an enlarged plan which showed spaces and numbers, but no key to explain the meaning of the numbers. I explained that this was only a plan of the ground floor as the upper floors had collapsed. For some time we discussed the following points:

- the relative sizes of spaces shown – if this were *not* a palace, what other type of building might it be?
- the black 'dots' (representing position of pillars) and speculation as to where the main entrance might be
- the types of use of the small spaces
- whether or not it was a palace.

The classroom discussion

This was not as 'neat and tidy' as planned, since I wanted to follow up and develop initiatives offered by the children.

The pupils' ideas and reasons for thinking that the Knossos building may or may not be a palace, as I noted them down during the discussion, are as follows:

'It could have been a smaller palace – for a lesser person than a king.'

'It's a large building and it must have been a palace.'

'It could have been a massive office such as tax office.'

'Maybe is was some type of museum – a place for collections.'

'I'm not certain it's a palace ... not sure what it is.'

'It could be a house of a rich man because it's not big enough to be a palace.'

'It could have been a prison...the labyrinth may have really been a prison.'

'It's a house, the lower floor for servants (the part Evans discovered), upper floor for family.'

'It could be a very big temple.'

'It may have been a burial chamber because small rooms are chambers where people are buried.'

'The entire building could have been the labyrinth.'

Labelling and keying the plan

In the second half of the session the class, working in groups, was asked to colour code the plan, saying what the different numbered spaces might have been used for, assuming that this was a plan of a palace. We had a fairly long lead-in discussion prior to the colour coding, which was necessary to help the pupils understand this complex plan. Reference was made back to their own palace plans drawn in the previous session.

Pupil responses

Some good ideas came from the pupils' work with groupings of related spaces, for example, the elongated spaces along the western side were associated with stables and coach or chariot houses. There was a major emphasis by some pupils on toilets and bathrooms, as indeed there had been on their own palace plans! Good use was made of stairway areas leading up to the missing first floor where some pupils assumed the more palatial parts of the palace may have been - a theory shared by Evans.

Session 5 Examining objects for clues about Knossos

Using a range of sources we moved on to try and bring the palace plan to life. Here the pupils were cast in the role of investigative historians, using questions about a variety of sources presented in a visual form to push on with their enquiry.

Learning objective

The learning objective for this session was to bring all aspects of an Ancient Greek palace to life.

Resources

The resources used in this session consisted of pictures of remains found at Knossos with questions written below them. Each was mounted on a separate sheet of paper.

The teaching

Pictures as clues

I began by referring back to the last session and to the children's ideas on what sort of building Evans might have discovered, for example, an office, the house of a rich man, a museum, temple, prison or burial chamber. I told the classes I had some pictures of objects which Arthur Evans discovered on the site of his 'Palace of Minos'. Perhaps, I suggested, these objects might provide clues about the purpose of the building.

Studying the clues

The class worked in small groups of between three and four pupils. The key question posed was *'What do these object clues tell you about the possible purpose and function of the building?'* Each group was given a set of seven pictures of objects Evans had found at Knossos. The pupils were first asked to jot down their ideas about each picture by answering the question written below each picture. As the pupils worked in groups the class teacher and I moved round amongst the children acting as their audience and where necessary clarifying the task I had set.

Comment on the discussion

The important teaching point here, I suggest, is to keep all options open rather than allowing the pupils to quickly close down the range of different ideas on the purpose of the building. If this seems to be happening, then it is useful for the teacher to produce questions to challenge an easy consensus.

A visit to Fishbourne Roman Palace

To bring Knossos to life, we were able to visit a Roman palace and use this as a subject for comparison. The two education officers at the palace provided a great deal of help and advice. The learning objectives of the visit were threefold: to see the ruins of what could have been a palace, to debate the use of such sites by looking at the evidence and to develop the pupils' understanding through their work in the role of archaeologists.

Illustrations 4 and 5: *Remains from Knossos*

Ancient Greece at Landscore Primary School
Introduction

Landscore School is a primary school with about 250 pupils on the outskirts of a small Devon town (population 10,000). The intake is drawn from both urban and rural areas and it covers the whole social spectrum. We taught the Ancient Greece HSU to two mixed (ability and gender) classes of Year 5 and Year 6 children. I worked closely with the two class teachers, Laura Austin and Graham Fisher. We taught the classes together, using genuine team teaching. The course lasted for fourteen weeks, on average half a day a week of one or two sessions. There was a considerable amount of follow-up time.

The purpose of teaching Ancient Greece

Our main goal in teaching Ancient Greece was to relate Ancient Greece to the modern world. This would be done through a range of activities drawing on the wonderfully varied and rich sources that survive.

Planning

The teachers of the two classes and I worked together as a team. In planning meetings before the term we discussed the best way of reconciling the History Study Unit's demands with how we would like to teach the topic. We decided to look at the idea of the legacy of Ancient Greece, and planned to start with questions to discover what the pupils already knew. We wanted the pupils to draw up their own concept webs based upon the HSU's headings.

Planning continued during the term with regular meetings to discuss progress and plan for future sessions. Each week we focused on a particular activity. The main emphasis was to be on the development of an understanding of Ancient Greek society and how it had evolved.

Resources

The teaching was well resourced. The school had a number of Ancient Greece teaching packs, book boxes from the library loan service and their own resources. In terms of information and source books, the following are particularly useful:

R Burrell and P Connolly, *The Greeks*. Oxford University Press, 1989.

J Crosher, *The Greeks*. MacDonald, 1981.

Homer, *The Odyssey*. Penguin, 1972.

M Gibson, *Gods, Men and Monsters*. Peter Lowe, 1977.

J Mason, S Peach and A Millard, *The Greeks*. Usborne, 1990.

A Pearson, *What do we know about the Greeks?* Simon and Schuster, 1992.

R Rees, *The Greeks*. Heinemann, 1994.

P Taylor, *The Ancient Greeks*. Heinemann, 1991.

Outline of the teaching programme

I went in on a regular weekly basis. Each week I spent a whole day in school, teaching two classes. The class teacher and I team-taught the lessons, having prepared a detailed lesson plan and organized the resources beforehand. As well as the class teacher, I worked closely with three third year B.Ed. students who came in to school each week. We taught one or two one and a half hour sessions a week, with a third, shorter, session of one hour with one of the two forms. For many sessions we combined the two classes.

Session 1 An Ancient Greek travel poster

In the opening lesson we decided to concentrate on the overall pattern of the HSU.

Planning

We had a long discussion on how to introduce the subject. We wanted to build on the children's existing knowledge. So, we would ask the children to develop their own concept map of modern Greece, and use this as the basis for studying Ancient Greece. But in order to introduce variety, we decided to modify the concept/topic web pattern by getting the pupils to work on the headings in a different way. The teaching idea we used is an old favourite: the children work in groups to produce a travel poster of a country using as their evidence travel brochures and topic books.

Learning objectives

The learning objectives for this session were simply to develop an understanding of the location and geography of Greece, including climate, scenery and agriculture and, through this activity, to build up an idea of what Ancient Greece was like.

Resources

Our resources for this session were:

- travel brochures, with lots of pictures of scenes of Greece, including sea, valleys, mountains, ancient buildings (from local travel agents – don't take too many from any one shop!)
- topic books on Ancient Greece
- large sheets of cartridge paper
- glue, scissors, marker pens

The teaching

The travel poster

We told the class that we were going to study Ancient Greece and that they were going to produce a travel poster about it. First we split the class up into pairs and they had to tell each other what they knew about Greece and jot down ideas. We then asked if any individuals in the class knew anything special. Luckily one pupil had lived in Greece, and had kept a large scrapbook. Immediately we engaged him in helping to answer questions from the whole class.

Pupils' questions

We now shifted the focus from finding out what they knew to encouraging them to ask questions. The children were grouped in pairs to draw up lists of questions about Ancient Greece. Each pair then volunteered a question which was listed on the board.

Preparing a poster

The pairs were then told that they had to produce posters or a display on Ancient Greece, using travel brochures and topic books, selecting from the brochure or topic books things that they thought had remained the same since Ancient Greek times.

Organizing the work

We put up a list of Study Unit headings for them to work on. The headings were:

- Where
- Climate
- Scenery
- Plains, hills, coasts
- Vegetation
- Farming
- Towns and cities
- Sport and leisure
- Religion
- Buildings

For each heading, each pair had to produce one piece of evidence from the brochures or the topic books, a title and a short statement or caption about it. They were also told that they must show no modern scenes, buildings or cars.

Working on the poster

Lots of heated discussion followed on how best to produce and present the posters. A rapid, frenetic tearing up of brochures and cutting out of information was followed by lots of gluing and sticking. For the rest of the week the class continued working on their posters. These were displayed, and a poster competition was held, with voting for the best poster.

Ancient Greek concept web

To reinforce what they had learned, the pupils were asked to create their own concept webs. We placed Ancient Greece at the centre, with linking words to the concept along the web's spokes.

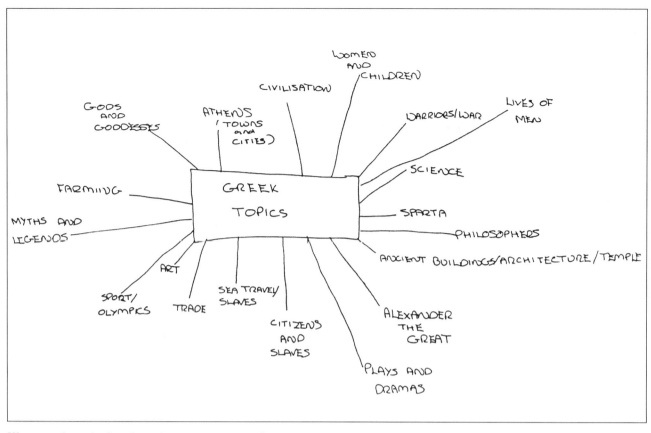

Illustration 6: *Pupil work – a concept web*

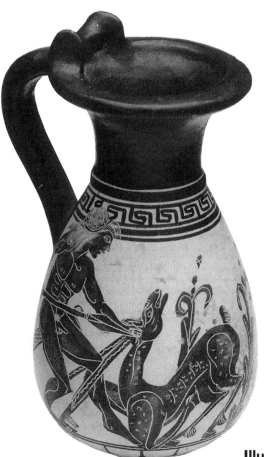

Having worked on an outline of the Ancient Greeks, we now focused on life in Ancient Greece through the study of a Greek pot, a present from a student who had picked it up passing through Athens airport.

A feature of the lesson was teaching the pupils how they can find out about another society from a single clue, in this case the jug.

We then used the information gleaned to create a table to reveal what the object told us about Greek society. The pupils worked in pairs on the questions to be considered, for example, *'What were the raw materials?'* We then pooled the answers on the board. Greek society began to unfold in front of us.

Illustration 7: *A little Greek jug*

Session 3 Classroom archaeologist

We aimed to involve our pupils in finding out about Ancient Greece and the nature of available evidence through the medium of an archaeology simulation. For the simulation we selected sources that showed the wide variety of available evidence. Uppermost in our minds was to reach the human beings behind the evidence, that is, to stress that each piece of evidence tells us something new about the Ancient Greeks.

Learning objectives

Our learning objectives were as follows:

- To introduce the idea of the archaeologist at work
- To present resource material in an interesting way
- To develop pupils' deductive and imaginative skills in handling pieces of evidence
- To teach them about Ancient Greek civilization
- To teach them about the evidence upon which we base our understanding of Ancient Greece

Resources

Before the lesson we had prepared a blank archaeological grid, and pictures of the remains the children were to find in each square. We had eight copies of this remains sheet, each cut up so that the pupils could stick what they found in the relevant square on the blank grid. We had also copied information from topic books, compiling a page of information about each square on the dig. (See illustrations 8 and 9.)

The Dig

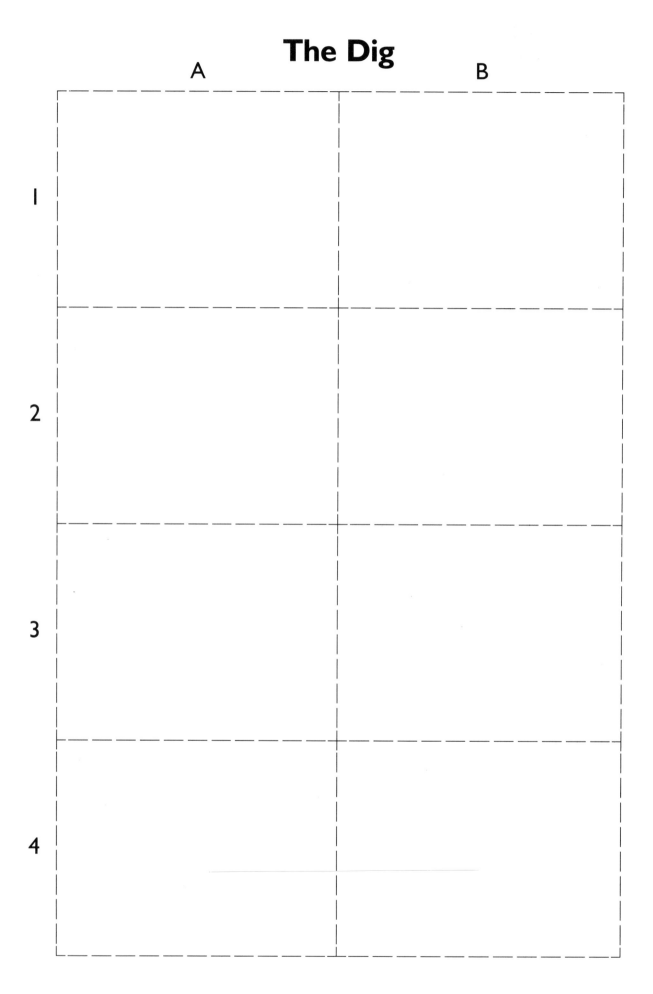

Illustration 8: *Blank archaeological dig grid*

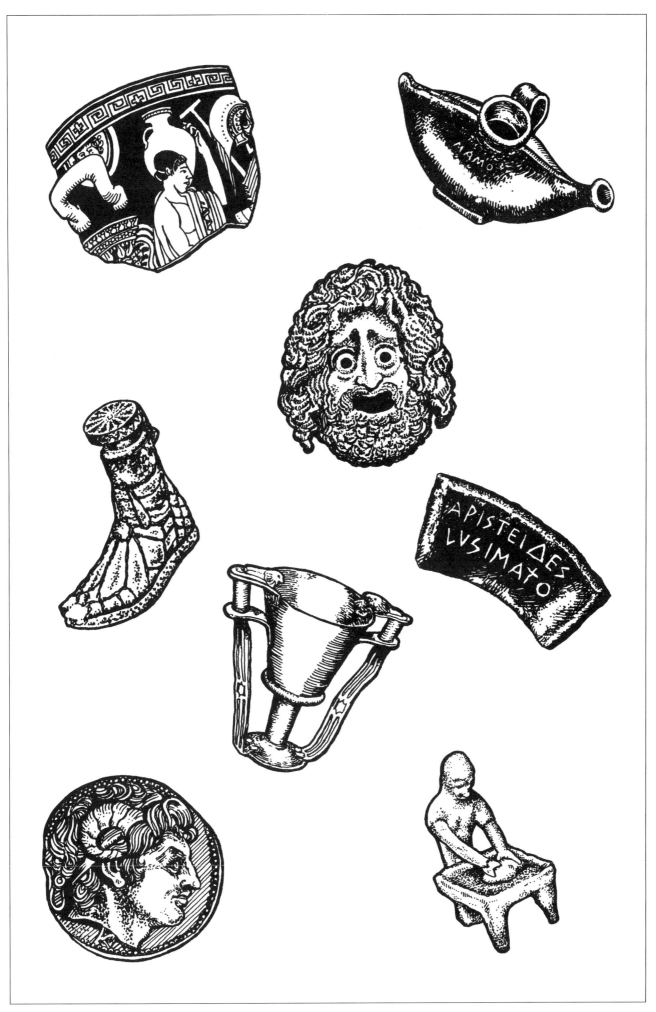

Illustration 9: *Objects to use with archaeological dig grid*

The teaching

We had a question and answer session about what an archaeologist is and how he/she goes about archaeological work and came up with this key question: *'If we are carrying out a dig, what questions do we need to ask before starting the excavation?'* One pupil commented that the archaeologist uses a grid to record finds, providing a perfect opportunity to introduce our grid. We also, I am sorry to say, tried the joke about an archaeologist being a person whose career lies in ruins. Nobody laughed.

Pupils work in pairs

We then split the class into pairs and threes, one sheet per pair or threesome. We told them that they were going to dig up the area shown on the grid. For each square excavated they would stick on to their grid a picture of what they had found.

Working as archaeologists: digging up the squares

There was much excitement as we gave the class the choice of which square to dig up. When the choice was made, the pupils engaged in animated discussion about what they had found and its significance. They used their topic books to find out more about the object that they had excavated.

We also gave them the research sheets prepared from the topic books. This worked well, as each group was able to report back something about what they had found. We pulled the class together to pool ideas and see where the discussion might lead. We continued digging until all eight squares were excavated. The pupils were able to record fully what they thought the objects to be.

Thinking about the evidence

The final idea was to put up the blank grid on the board and get the class to say what kind of evidence it was that we had produced.

Story time

We had planned to use the evidence from the grid work to tell a story, but ran out of time. Our lesson outline for this further development of the grid results is as follows:

- each pair think up a story about the site, based on the evidence
- each tells their story in two or three sentences
- each story summed up on the board in a single phrase/sentence
- buzz words – brainstorm a list of these for the story chosen to be elaborated on.

We moved on to examine the idea of myth, the origins of Ancient Greece and the evidence upon which our knowledge and understanding of Ancient Greece is based. While telling the story we got the children to draw the scenes.

Translation of ideas from spoken to visual form

I gave each pupil a blank piece of A4 paper folded into four rectangles. We told them that as each of the eight scenes unfolded, (four on the front, four on the back) they would have to draw a picture of it in one of the eight spaces. They could give each a title and a caption.

The story in eight scenes

The King of Athens in Greece had to send seven young men and seven young women to the King of Crete each year to pay for the death of the son of the King of Crete whom the Athenians had killed. The fourteen children were fed to the Minotaur who lived in a maze below the Cretan king's palace.

1 The King of Athens' son was called Theseus. Theseus was a fierce warrior, who had killed all his enemies. He said he would sail to Crete as one of the children to be sacrificed.
2 The chosen children boarded the ship. The ship sailed to Crete. Theseus said it would have a white sail if it returned to Athens safely with the children.
3 They landed in Crete and were taken to the king. King Minos' daughter Ariadne fell in love with Theseus.
4 In the middle of the night she gave Theseus a ball of string and a dagger.
5 Next day he was taken to the maze and killed the monster.
6 That night Ariadne went to his room, and Theseus escaped with her and the other children.
7 Theseus and Ariadne had a quarrel. So Theseus left Ariadne on a convenient island.
8 He sailed home, but forgot to put up the white sail, so his father, the King of Athens, threw himself off a cliff. Theseus then became King of Athens.

Storytelling

In telling the story of the Minotaur, I made sure that I painted the scene thoroughly with the tramp of boots, crying mothers and Theseus and the captain standing together on the deck of the boat. When it came to the killing of the Minotaur I had a child take the part of the Minotaur, with Theseus feeling his way through the dark, making for the roars of the monster. A swift struggle, a stabbing and the monster lay dead. The children responded with gusto as I told the story, the quicker ones having time to put titles and captions on each picture they drew.

Story telling, like all teaching skills, needs both nerve and practice. Advice on how to launch into this extremely rewarding method can be found in the NPHP companion volume *Teaching Primary History*.

In Session 5, we introduced a modern interpretation in the form of a feature film. We used this to compare with the myth we had studied.

Session 6 Greek architecture

We moved on to Greek architecture. Greek architecture has had an impact on all of us through its continuous influence on the design of buildings. A combination of local study and a planning simulation seemed a good way of getting this across to our pupils. Luckily there were a number of local buildings in a classical style within a five minute walk of our classroom. As the weather was fine, we decided to take the two classes down into the town to do some sketching of suitable buildings.

Learning objectives In this session, we wanted to:

- introduce pupils to the ideas of Greek architecture
- give them some insight into the minds of the Greeks and their architects
- develop powers of observation and recording
- give them some insight into how Greek ideas have influenced building in Britain.

Resources We had some lovely posters of Greek and Greek-style buildings, in particular a sun-drenched Parthenon and a damp-looking British Museum, as well as an illustration of features of Ancient Greek buildings. We also used:

- the locality
- clipboards for local sketching
- squared paper.

The teaching

Features of Greek architecture

The pupils were told before we started that we would be looking for certain features. These would be triangles, rectangles, circles, pillars and squares. We also examined and discussed the kinds of columns the Ancient Greeks used and how they decorated their pediments and friezes. We then told the class that we were going out to the town to draw and label these features as they appeared on buildings.

Using large pictures

Before going into the town centre, we gathered the children round, sitting them on desks and the floor, and got them to point out the features on the posters of the Parthenon and the British Museum. We asked questions about why and how buildings were designed, for example, why would a temple's plan take that particular form? We chose an artistic child to draw the shapes of the façade on the board. The children then drew and labelled their own elevations of the buildings.

The field work

The classes were then divided into two groups. One group ended up at the Methodist Chapel, and happily drew for ten minutes, getting down the main outlines of the building. We concentrated on making sure that they had the shapes clearly drawn, and that they were labelled. Each pupil was able to come back to school with a building made up of triangles, rectangles, circles and squares, plus pillars. They were also aware of the order and relationship between the different shapes.

Session 7 An Ancient Greek burger bar: planning a building

This session was based on the concept of pupils planning a building in an Ancient Greek style for an architectural contest. We seized on the idea of designing a burger bar, knowing it would be popular with the children. Also, a local fast food restaurant, although modern, used Greek decorative motifs.

Learning objective

The learning objective for this session was to develop an understanding of how and why the Greeks might have designed a building.

Resources

We designed a template sheet and costing plan for the children to use in planning out their buildings (see Illustrations 10 and 11).

GREEK BURGER BAR TEMPLE

You are taking part in a **contest** to build a Greek burger bar.

Your job is to **design** the front of the building so it looks like a Greek temple.

To help you, look at **ruins** of Greek temples and **buildings** built like them since. Work out how they are planned.

Below are the **main shapes** you will use. By each is what it will cost to build **all or part** of a **square** for that shape using your planning grid.

Each square represents one metre.
The burger bar will be **15 metres wide** and **15 metres high** from the ground to the top of the roof.

Shape	Cost per square	no of squares used	cost
Pillars or columns	2		
Head of pillars	2 plain 6 decorated		
Pediment	2		
Architrave	3		
Base	1		
Frieze	6		
Statues	50		
Total cost of our temple facade			

Illustration 11: *Costing plan for Greek burger bar*

GREEK TEMPLE SHAPES

Head of Pillars

Pillars or Columns

Pediment

Frieze stuck on front of pediment

Architrave

Base

Illustration 10: *Greek temple shapes template*

The teaching

Linking into local knowledge

We started off asking how many of the class had been into the McDonald's in Exeter. Almost all of the form replied 'yes'. We asked what they had noticed about the decoration. 'White' was one answer. Someone else said 'pillars' and then someone remarked 'Ancient Greek architecture'. 'Greek decorations' was also heard. We called a pupil up to draw its features on the blackboard and she made a good job of drawing the columns.

Patterns and buildings

Now we moved on to looking at the idea of the shapes we had worked out from the Parthenon picture in the morning. We looked at it again. Questioning followed a normal path: *'Where is it ?'* – Athens. *'What is it ?'* Carrie was asked to come out and demonstrate the shapes that we had noticed this morning. This reinforced the ideas we were developing, but very consciously in terms of working off the evidence. We were able to point out the triangle, the heads of the columns, the general rectangular shape, the architrave, and so on.

Planning the building

Now we moved on to the activity, which was to design a burger bar to look like a Greek temple. We handed out the temple template sheet plus a sheet of information showing a cut away picture of the Parthenon, details of the gods and how to put together stones and columns. The templates were to be used on gridded paper with the same size squares. We decided the temple would be 15 metres long and 15 metres high, with each grid square representing one square metre.

Pupils work in pairs

We split the pupils up into pairs. We then went over what planning was required, and how big their temple front had to be. Ideas about decoration were shared. The pupils had to plan, label and justify their designs. They then got on with their work. Victoria, a special needs pupil, was interesting to observe, in that she was able to assemble and stick the labels onto the shapes we cut out. By the end of the afternoon, all the pupils had completed the task, at least in outline. There was a really splendid and imaginative collection of responses. The follow-up was maths work on how much the burger bar would cost to build (see Illustration 11).

The next week there was a supply teacher for this group. She looked at the children's work and said, 'My husband is an architect. In our kids' room we have designed a cupboard, with a decoration on the front. We have done it like an Ancient Greek temple ... ' It was one of the best moments of the project.

Session 8 The Greek gods 1

How could we help the pupils learn about the Greek gods? What do we want them to learn? For a start, the information includes the idea that they lived for ever, that they lived on top of Mount Olympus, that they had their own hell, that there were a lot of them, that they had different jobs, that they got up to all kinds of crazy things and that we learn about them through stories handed down from generation to generation. What a lot to think about!

Planning

Our planning focused on the idea of story, with reference to five elements built around this theme. We started off with the concept that ancient societies had gods to meet their needs. If so, *what kinds of gods* would they have? The children would then *read about the gods*, using a common text. After this they would move into pairs and whole class activity, in which the pupils would have to *find out about the gods*. They would *use this information* to work out a pyramid structure to design a frieze for the front of their burger bar. We would *end with storytelling*, with the pupils making up a story from the scenes given them, and presenting it to the rest of the class. We would say that the scenes were fragments of a story which had been lost – they need to fill in the gaps. The storytelling element can be a separate lesson if time is short.

Learning objectives

The learning objectives for this session reflected the thinking outlined above. We wanted our pupils

- to develop some understanding of the Greek gods
- to relate this understanding to the main form of evidence which survives about the Greek gods, that is, stories and sculpture.

Resources

The resources for this session were a pyramid shape to use in making the pediment frieze for the burger bar (see Illustration 10) and cut-out figures of the gods with potted biographies, in envelopes, one per envelope.

ZEUS

Zeus became the chief of the gods. He was god of the sky, storms, thunder and lightning. Zeus ruled from Olympus and his symbols include the eagle, the oak tree and thunderbolts.

HERA

Hera was the sister and wife of Zeus. She was the goddess of marriage and childbirth. Hera was very angry when Zeus had affairs and children with other women. Her symbols are the pomegranate and the peacock.

POSEIDON

Poseidon was the brother of Zeus. He was god of the sea and also controlled storms at sea and sea monsters. Poseidon kept to himself in his underwater palace. His symbols are the trident, dolphins and horses.

DEMETER

Demeter was the goddess of farming, crops and other plants. She caused the winter by ignoring the plants while she searched for her kidnapped daughter, Persephone. Spring came when Persephone returned. Demeter's symbol is a sheaf of grain.

HERMES

Hermes was one of the sons of Zeus. His job was to be messenger of the gods and to take the souls of the dead to the underworld. Hermes was also the god of thieves. His symbols are his winged helmet and sandals.

ARTEMIS

Artemis was one of the daughters of Zeus. Her twin brother was the god, Apollo. She was goddess of the moon, hunting and wild animals. Her symbols are the cypress tree, dogs and deer.

ATHENE

Athene was one of the daughters of Zeus. Zeus swallowed her mother, the Titaness Metis, so that they would not have a son, since legends said that such a son would overthrow him. Athene was born from Zeus's head when he had it split open to get rid of a headache. She was the goddess of war and wisdom and also the patron deity of Athens. Her symbols are the owl and the olive tree.

APOLLO

Apollo was one of the sons of Zeus. His twin sister was the goddess, Artemis. Apollo was the god of light, thought, music and poetry. People thought that Apollo could predict the future. His symbol is the laurel tree.

Illustration 12: *Sample sheet of pictures and information on Greek gods*

The teaching

Questions about the gods

The first session opened with both classes sitting round the flip chart. I introduced the concept of the gods meeting the needs of people by asking what two different gods I would want to help me succeed when I go fishing (my hobby) and help deal with the problem of our sick cat. The pupil response was a god of water, plus the god of sickness to help the cat.

What kinds of gods might the Greeks need?

I told them that we were going to work on the Greek gods, and asked them to think about the kinds of gods the Greeks needed. What kinds of gods would they have worshipped if they had been a tribe of settlers who reached Ancient Greece over 2500 years ago? Also, where would the gods have lived, how long would they have lived, and what would they have done?

Problem solving in pairs

When the class understood what they were looking for, we split them into pairs. Each pair had to come up with three gods needed by a tribe who had come down to settle in Greece – a hunter and gatherer society. We then pooled ideas on the flip chart, ably assisted by a pupil who worked as the recorder. We ended up with two sides of gods!

Finding out about the gods

In the classroom the children started to work in pairs. We told them that they had to find out about the Greek gods from each other. Each pair had a picture of a Greek god and some information in an envelope. Then one of the pair stayed 'at home' while the second had in turn to interview the other pupils about their gods, finding out the gods' names and jobs. To do this we had folded A4 paper into eight, giving sixteen rectangles to fill in. At half time we swapped, the second child going around finding information, the other one 'at home'.

One of the aims of this session was to plan a frieze for the burger bar, showing the gods. After the various pairs had found out about the gods, they continued by planning their frieze, either as a family tree or as a story. The children were focused and enthusiastic, and a good time was had by all.

Having acquainted the children with the Greek gods, we now brought them to life through the medium of story. This was a story with a difference, because the children were going to create their own tale. We taught two groups the same lesson, one in the morning, the other in the afternoon, using the story of Actaeon. In our planning we abandoned the idea of giving the children the entire story to start with, instead asking them to work in groups on individual extracts from the myth.

Learning objectives

We wanted to engage the children's minds with the kind of thinking that underlay the Greeks' beliefs about their gods, stories that we now regard as myths.

Resources

We worked out some headings for a story about the Greek gods, and prepared a set of readings that told the story of Actaeon. The story was divided up into parts, some easier than others.

The teaching

Stories: the oral tradition

We talked about stories being handed down from generation to generation, these particular stories forming the basis of our knowledge of the Greek gods. We then told them that they would work on one such story.

We gave out differentiated extracts, telling the class that those passages were fragments of a lost story. In reading their extracts we followed our usual procedure for reading documents (see the NPHP book, *Teaching Primary History*). Having read and talked to each other about their extract, each group had to tell the rest of the class what their piece was about, and dramatize their part of the story. Each group came to the front to do this. Thus when the story we were using stated that the goddess, Artemis, was bathing in the nude, it was acted out with a tall girl as Artemis, while other girls tried to screen her from Actaeon's view. Actaeon was then turned into a deer, and the children showed the dogs chasing him and tearing him to pieces. This worked well and the whole class was fully involved, enjoying the acting out and retelling of the story.

In the afternoon we taught the same lesson, but with a different emphasis. Instead of giving the pupils the extracted pieces we asked them to choose according to how they felt about their reading. This went better as there was a better match between the pieces and the pupils' ability to work on them. The report back from the groups went very well, with a good level of attention and the acting as we went along gave the whole thing a tremendous dynamic.

Writing stories

In both sessions we gave the groups the story headings sheet. Each had to order the headings to work out a logical story using the scenes in the extracts as a starting point.

We stressed that their story should:

- have a plot, and a story line
- build up their descriptions of the characters
- try and paint the scenes as fully as they could, noting what they could see, hear, smell.

We encouraged the children to jot down words and phrases, to work in rough on paper and to explore ideas through talking. We said that they should not worry about the spelling and grammar at this stage; this would be looked at in the later stages of the writing. The exploration and development of ideas was the vital point. Later, each group was given time to present their story, acting out the scenes that they were describing. The stories were then written up in rough books, revised and presented neatly for display on the classroom walls.

Session 10 Blockbusters on Ancient Greece

Laura Austin's class had to present a whole school assembly and she came up with the idea of playing a game similar to Blockbusters with the whole school, using the theme of Ancient Greece. This appealed to all the children in the class who then set to work, each pupil producing a hexagon on an Ancient Greek topic with the question and the correct information to answer it. This Blockbusters-type game turned out to be an excellent way of covering factual information in the Ancient Greece History Study Unit.

Some of the topics covered in the game were:

religion	food	travel
warfare	trade	Alexander the Great
city-states	architecture	art
philosophers	myths	women's lives
scientists	children's lives	democracy
writers	theatre / plays	Crete
Olympics / sport	language	farming

1 Divide into two teams

2 Have ready a large board of white hexagons. Label them with the Ancient Greece topics you have decided on. Also have ready coloured hexagons in two colours.

3 Each side should have questions ready to ask the other team, divided into the topics chosen.

4 Taking turns, each side will choose a topic and get asked a question. If they are right, then that space becomes their colour.

5 The first team to get a correct line of their colour across the board wins.

6 You can choose hexagons to block your opponents! (This can be played using an overhead projector and coloured hexagon-shaped overlays.)

Illustration 13: *Ancient Greece Blockbusters instructions*

Session 11 Greek art: pottery

Greek pottery seemed a natural way in to the study of Greek art, and the information art can provide about Greek life, as there are so many scenes of everyday life on Greek pots. We wanted the children to design, make and decorate their own pots. For Laura's class we shifted from pots to the creation of hexagonal tiles, using the same set of ideas. We used the idea of tessellation to fit into the maths work which a colleague had been doing with both classes. Each pupil's brief was to make something to be sold at a tourist shop selling plates and vases, showing in the work as many different aspects of Greek life as possible.

Learning objectives

The learning objectives in this session were to learn as much as possible about Greek life from the pictures on their own newly created pottery, to analyse their pictures, to produce original designs using the Ancient Greek references as the basis for their work and to work in clay to better understand the skills and processes involved in producing Greek pots.

Resources

The resources used were as follows:

- Books on Ancient Greece and sheets of pictures and information. Each pupil needs access to at least one pictorial source sheet.
- Well-sharpened pencils, coloured pencils and crayons.
- Greek pottery research sheets, enough for the whole class.

GREEK POTTERY

Pupil's name_____

What kind of pot is it?

plate   jug   cup   bowl   vase   dish   urn   storage pot   (circle)

What might it have been used for? _____

_____

What does the picture on the pot show? (one or two words) _____

_____

Where did you find out about your pot, if you know?

Name of author of book _____

Book's title_____

_____ page_____

Quick sketch (below or overleaf)

Do a quick sketch of your pot. Make sure you show its

        shape   subject   decoration (if any)

Illustration 14: *Greek pottery research sheet*

The teaching

Studying Greek pots

We told the children that we were going to study Greek vases and plates, using the example of the little Greek jug, (see page 18). We explained that we were doing this in order to find out what we can about how the Ancient Greeks lived, and that we were going to use this knowledge to design our own plates, vases and jugs for a tourist shop.

Picture of a Greek pot

We pinned up on the blackboard a large picture, poster size, of a vase showing women carrying water. Each pupil came up with three facts or things that they could see and a lively questioning session then ensued in which we teased out how the women in the picture would have been dressed. Graham had some saris, so we used these to dress up two girls along the lines of the women in the picture. The children worked out and organized how the girls looked. We asked what other things Ancient Greeks would have worn, working from the pictorial evidence.

Designing pots

The children were asked, working from their knowledge of Ancient Greece, what kinds of things would they expect to see on their plates, vases, jugs and storage pots? We brainstormed possible ideas and then asked for three volunteers, and with blackboard pens they scribbled away furiously, putting up a list of ideas on the board.

What was really interesting was the continuing impact of the previous blockbusters game work. Laura's class had done it, but Graham's hadn't. Graham's class had no real set of good ideas about Greek life in general, and were therefore limited to the topics we had done, while Laura's class had a broad area of knowledge to work from.

Researching using information sheets

We told the children that they were going to research into Greek pots. They would choose one pot each from the topic books and other resources provided.

We handed out the research sheets, and explained how they were to be filled in. Together, on the blackboard, we worked through an example. By the end of the lesson all of the class had been able to extract one picture and scene of Greek life.

Designing a vase

Graham's class then prepared designs for their own vases on the subject they had researched. We used pictures of a full range of pots to work out five main categories: plate, bowl, vase, dish, jug. The children then chose one of these shapes to design their own pots.

Designing and making tiles

For Laura's class, it was decided that we would get them to design tiles instead of making pots, building on the blockbusters hexagon idea. Also, we felt that we could actually make tiles in the school pottery; Greek pots might be more difficult!

For this session we went on to look at Greek travel. It became the focus of the teaching for the second half of the term. I had come up with the idea of designing and making a board game, but the problem was simply that Greek travel, as travel, was really rather dull – they sailed boats, rowed, walked, rode on donkeys and so on. Then I stumbled on the glaringly obvious – why not build it around the voyage of Odysseus and other episodes in the Greek myths that involved travel, in particular the adventures of Oedipus? The accounts of travel, in the *Odyssey* and in the Oedipus myth, were written during the Ancient Greek period. So we decided upon a combined approach, teaching Ancient Greek travel through the medium of story, complete with the design of a board game. In our teaching of this topic we worked with two students, Pam and Jackie.

Learning objectives

The learning objectives for these sessions were as follows:

- To learn as much as possible about Greek travel, and the problems found by travellers, using the available evidence, but in particular focusing on myths and legends.
- To develop creative skills through producing board games.
- To develop descriptive language skills by producing stories and poems.
- To develop understanding through story, linked in to the creation of a board game.
- By retelling the *Odyssey* stories, to encourage the use of imagination linked in to all the faculties – smell, taste, touch, hearing, sight.

Resources

We prepared resources in the form of travel cards, to illustrate the problems that travellers faced. The written sources came from the *Odyssey* and the story of Theseus (Illustration 15).

We also provided topic books containing information on Greek travel, posters depicting Greek artefacts and books on Greek myths and legends, particularly the Trojan War, the *Odyssey* and Theseus and the Minotaur.

The teaching

Going on a holiday

The morning session was spent encouraging the children to get to grips with the idea of a story built around travel, involving a range of adventures. Jackie got the children to shut their eyes and think of their last holiday or long journey.

They had to think of what it involved, and what could have happened. We asked them to think about exciting, interesting, horrible things that they have heard about people travelling. These were recorded on the board.

Working in pairs, they told each other about personal journeys and holidays, and answered each other's questions. Next we asked them to draw a cartoon of their holiday journey, using A4 paper folded into eight rectangles, a scene for each rectangle. The cartoons had a title, 'Holiday adventure', and a caption. On the board we listed scenes for them to include in their cartoons : getting ready / leaving / the journey / arriving / the holiday / packing up / going home. Each pupil then came to the front of the class to tell their story.

Cartoon display

We planned to collect in their cartoons and display them on a timeline, so that the other pupils could then find out about their holidays and the things that can happen. As usual, we ran out of time. The lesson went exactly as we had planned, with superb descriptions of a wide range of holidays.

The next session introduced the idea of the board game but focused on teasing out the evidence about travel in Ancient Greek times. The same 'core' work was done with two classes. One was to focus on research through creating board games, the other through developing stories.

The teaching

Creating a board game

We told the children that they were going to produce a board game about travel in Greek times or a traveller's story. We would have to base these on what we could find out about the Ancient Greeks. With one class we asked the children to bring in board games to use as models for the teaching during the following lessons.

Map work

We handed out the Greek map (Illustration 1) and a resource sheet on Greek travel, one between two children. We told the class that we were going to make up our board game based on the adventures of a famous Greek traveller, Odysseus, who would be going from Ithaca to Troy and back again. The children then had to find these places on the map and put their fingers on them, and work out a possible route from Ithaca to Troy.

Dramatic re-enactment: the story of Helen

Now we told the story of Helen being carried off to Troy, and dramatized it with two of the pupils taking the roles of Helen and Paris. We got the class, in role as Agamemnon and the Achaeans [Greeks], to work out what we could do to get her back. We told the story of the siege of Troy to the point where the siege was over, and Odysseus was the hero of the Wooden Horse saga. Then we introduced the idea of Odysseus travelling back home to Ithaca.

Problem solving	The next task was to use our various resources to work out the kinds of problems Odysseus might have had travelling from Troy to Ithaca. The pupils studied the map, noting the large number of islands, the difficulty of working out a route back to Ithaca from Troy and the problems which this might cause. They had to think about both land and sea travel. In pairs, the pupils had to present at least three problems, and how they might have solved them. They had to think of:

- the distances travelled
- the time taken, allowing for an average of ten kilometres a day
- the difficulties that the weather could cause.

Pooling ideas: star diagram/concept web	As a class we pooled ideas, and drew on the board a star diagram of the problems which the pupils thought travellers might face, with the corollary that this should tie into the game. The list included: frostbite, wet socks, toes dropped off, Africa, eaten by crocodiles, being taken hostage, strange animals, war and prisoners, accidents, swimming, discovering new lands. They all copied this list into their rough books.
Introducing the *Odyssey*	We explained that there are many stories about Greek travel. The most famous story is the *Odyssey* of Homer. Homer wrote the *Odyssey* hundreds of years after Odysseus's journey. Odysseus had many adventures, which we would find out about from the *Odyssey* – it contains lots of clues about Greek travel. We would imagine that we were with Odysseus – his guardian angel, or in this case one of the gods, Athene. We also used other stories to think about what might have happened on his journey. Another famous story is about the journey of Oedipus, extracts from which we had cut up and mounted.
Problems travellers faced	We wanted to extend the list of difficulties and add to it ideas from the *Odyssey* and the Oedipus myth. We therefore prepared a list of topics with extracts from the *Odyssey* and the Oedipus myth to illustrate the particular difficulties an Ancient Greek traveller might have encountered.
Graded sources	We had graded the source sheets for difficulty, using colour coding. On one side of the sheet was an extract from the Odyssey, on the other a picture of a scene reflecting the kind of travel in the extract. We marked the source sheets easy, medium and hard. We gave the groups (pairs or threes) the chance to choose which they would prefer. For some even the easiest reading proved too hard; we should have included some which were easier still.
Pupils teaching the class	We wanted the class to pool its ideas and solutions to problems. So, having now their readings and problems to solve, we told the pupils that they would each have to prepare a report to teach the rest of the

class about their findings. The task each pupil had was broken down into stages. They had to:

- read the story
- write some notes from which to report to the rest of the class
- make their report to class

We said that certain scenes would be acted out in front of the class. This we did at the end of the lesson using the 'hot seat' approach. It proved to be an active lesson which covered a huge amount of ground and left us with the chance to carry on next time with the board game.

CYCLOPS	SACKING A TOWN – A BATTLE
SIRENS	CIRCE–TURNED INTO PIGS
SCYLLA & CHARYBDIS	SHIPWRECK
LANDS IN ITHACA	A STORM
TRAVEL ON A CART	LAUNCHING A SHIP
THE LOTUS EATERS	AMBUSHED IN A TOWN
FOG	SHIP STRIKES A ROCK
SCYLLA & CHARYBDIS – THE WHIRLPOOL AND TIDE-RACE	LAND TRAVEL – ATTACKED WITH A CLUB
LAND TRAVEL – TORN APART BY PINE TREES	LAND TRAVEL – FIGHT ON A CLIFF EDGE
LAND TRAVEL – THE PROCRUSTEAN BED	ROCKS FALL INTO THE SEA

Illustration 15: *Ancient Greece travel cards*

Having done the background research, we were now ready to plan out the games or create the story.

Learning objective

The learning objective for these sessions was, through the process of creating a game or writing a story, to develop and deepen an understanding of travel in Ancient Greece. Here we will focus on Graham's class and their board games.

Resources

The resources we used were as follows:

- card, pens, pencils, glue, paper
- existing board games
- resource cards
- outline map of Ancient Greece (see Illustration 1).

The teaching

We started off the lesson with the children working on the cards which they had had the previous week, writing a short summary and presenting this to the rest of the class. The need for them to think about public speaking was positive, with us advising them on how to speak – good, deep breath, head and chin up, look at the class, speak slowly and loudly, and so on.

Analysis of existing games

We then talked about games, and put up on the board a list of the kinds of games that they knew, using three headings.

map/board	aim	choices
Monopoly	get money	chance and community cards, buying property
Cluedo	guess who was murdered	clue cards

Having gone through a number of examples, and got across the concept, we laid down the pattern for the game.

Guidelines for making a board game

The pupils came up with the following terms of reference for a board game:

- it could be a board or a map
- it needed research, based on what they could find out about Ancient Greece

- each game had to pass through four places: Troy, Sparta, Knossos and Athens, with the point of the game being the voyage of Odysseus from Troy to his home in Ithaca.

Structuring the group work	The task required pupils to stick to a plan which involved:

- research
- planning the game
- designing the board, based on the Greek map
- writing the rules, chance cards, briefing

The **rules** would reflect what the pupils knew about Greek travel. The **chance cards** must be based on something they had read or found out about the Ancient Greeks, and the **briefing** would give a full account of what the game intended to show, and link it into Greek history.

We were very conscious of the need to give specific children specific tasks that would force them to cooperate. The pupils were split into friendship groups. Each group had a maximum of four people. Each pupil was given a specific role. Each group was told to appoint a person in charge, so that person could report back ideas to the rest of the class after fifteen minutes. There were ten groups in all. At the end of the session we collected in the work from each group, storing it in individual folders made of cartridge paper. |
| **Continuing the work** | The class continued working for several sessions on its board games, with the B.Ed. students helping investigate, research, extract and organize information and present it in the form of board games. One of their classroom diaries reads, 'The work continued on the board games – pairs or groups continued to plan their games and started to make them. It was interesting to see how various groups worked. Some worked as a whole group, while others split into pairs and worked on separate tasks, in some cases individuals did their own thing and pooled their results.' One problem was that some groups were more interested in developing a game and lost sight of the goal, learning about Greek travel. |
| **Playing the games** | The day when the games would be played arrived and all but two of the games were finished in time. Laura's class came, having been invited in to 'test play' the games. 'These are really good', was one overheard comment. The general consensus of opinion was that Laura's class was green with envy at what the other class had achieved. What the class had produced *was* astounding, ranging in sophistication from the simple to the complex. |

Greek science

With the end of term approaching and our board games played and stories told, we had a week to spare. So why not look at Greek science? We decided to give the children three problems to solve: the measuring of the earth's circumference, the lifting of water from one level to another and the mystery of the king's crown.

Learning objectives

The learning objectives for these sessions were to develop an understanding that the Greeks produced some great thinkers and scientists, and to help the pupils to share the thinking processes of the Greek scientists.

Resources

The resources we used were as follows:

- a set of screws
- containers
- objects
- lead weights
- atomic scale

The teaching

Greek thinkers and scientists

We told the class that the Greeks were famous for their thinkers, mathematicians, scientists, philosophers. The most famous were the philosophers Plato and Aristotle, the mathematicians Euclid and Pythagoras and the inventor and scientist, Archimedes.

Problem solving

We would be trying to solve three problems which the Greeks had solved: measuring how far it is round the earth, the lifting of water and the problem of the crown.

Problem 1: measuring the earth's circumference

Our first problem was measuring the circumference of the earth. The Ancient Greeks knew the earth was round, and had a good idea of its size. We told the children that to try and solve their problem they would have the following resources, and nothing else:

- pencils and paper
- a protractor to measure angles
- two thirty-metre-high poles. The two poles are five hundred miles apart and on a north-south axis, the sun is shining on them and it is midday.

Pair work

The class worked in pairs or small groups, to produce their ideas of how to solve the problem. Their answers varied, but were mostly guesswork, as they had no idea of how to solve the problem of measuring the earth's circumference.

Feeding in ideas and information	Then we fed in clues to help them solve the problem. We started with the idea of the angle which the sun gave at midday in two places five hundred miles apart, one of these points being on the equator. We managed to work out that the first angle would be 90 degrees. We then told the class that the second angle the Greeks had measured was 82.5 degrees.
	We could then draw a triangle, the base being five hundred miles. As a class we worked out that the angle at the top of the triangle would be the angle which represented that percentage of the earth's circumference. The angle at the top of the triangle was 7.5 degrees. We divided 360 degrees by 7.5 and multiplied that answer (48) by 500. A magic moment, as we came up with a very correct-looking answer: 24,000 miles!
Problem 2: lifting water	How can you lift water from one level to another without using a bucket or a lever? This is a problem that the Greek scientist Archimedes faced. On the board we drew a cross section showing the river and the canal, with a metre between their water height levels.
Pair work	Again the children worked in groups or pairs to solve Archimedes' problem. After some time to consult, we asked each group to explain their ideas to teachers. These included a water wheel, a pump, a dam, lowering the ground, gravity, suction, digging the ditch to meet the river. One pair even suggested having a screw-shaped pipe, (probably a half-remembered idea triggered by the name Archimedes), driven by a donkey. The pair decided to use the donkey to turn a handle, and to do this through the use of gears – a transfer of ideas from previous work on cogs.
	We then gave each group a clue, a picture of an Archimedes screw to look at. Back to work they went, and one pair solved it straight away. Having sorted out their idea of an Archimedes screw, each group drew one in their rough books, and were then given a sheet to do a neat drawing of their machine, with labels and a caption of how it might work.
Problem 3: Archimedes and the crown	We next told the story of the king who felt sure that he was being swindled. His jewellers told him that his crown was made of solid gold and, although it looked as if it was gold, one of his spies told the king that his jewellers used a lot of lead in making the crown, covering the lead with gold. The king was desperate to know the truth, so he called in Archimedes to help solve the problem. I asked Graham to be king and he found a remarkable gold, starry object to wear as a crown. I was the scientist summoned to his presence. We pretended that the king would kill me if I could not solve the problem of whether the crown was made of pure gold or devalued by lead added to it.

I came up with some ideas, and begged the class to help save my life. The idea of melting the crown down led to the class howling that it would end in my death. During this discussion the idea of weighing the bulk of the crown against an equal volume of gold surfaced. Then I said that I was hot and sticky with worry and would go home and have a bath, making a lot of being fat and the water rising when I got in. I then acted out the scene of running from the bath, shouting 'Eureka! Eureka!'

Classroom experiment

Again, the pupils got into groups to try and work out how I had solved the problem of the crown. They eventually came up with the idea of gold displacing a different amount of water than the same weight of lead. We then brought in a couple of buckets, and managed to immerse objects made of different materials, measuring the amount of water they displaced. The water was then weighed in a container, using an accurate weighing machine.

Ancient Greece at Midhurst Intermediate School
Introduction

Midhurst Intermediate School for 7–12 year olds stands on the outskirts of Midhurst in West Sussex. The class to whom I taught Ancient Greece contained 28 Year 6 children, some very bright, some average, some a little below average.

The sessions taught were an ambitious attempt to investigate how the Ancient Greeks thought about life and death, democracy and science through the eyes of selected Ancient Greek writers, a particularly challenging set of ideas for both teachers and pupils. Clearly the concepts involved would prove difficult for some of the children whose literary skills were weak. In teaching the class I worked closely with the class teacher, Tony Hopkins.

Session 1 Introducing Ancient Greece

Challenge is very much what the NPHP project is about, and when I came to look for sources I returned constantly to a collection I had already used when working with teachers. It seemed to me to contain material that was designed to make you think hard about what the Greeks stood for, and if the information was right for adults, then with a little modification it should prove right for children.

Learning objectives

The learning objectives of this session were to enable the children to question sources and to understand that we were dealing with a distant time and that the reconstructions we see in museums, on sites and in books are no more, in some cases, than educated guesses.

Resources

The resource used in this session was the famous fresco of two boys boxing, which I cut up to remove all the modern infill reconstruction, leaving a jigsaw of about twelve pieces.

Illustration 16: *Boxing boys fresco*

The teaching

The puzzle

I explained to the children that the pieces they each had represented about one quarter of the reconstructed fresco. Could they, without looking at the archaeologist's reconstruction, make their own? They readily agreed and promised to have it ready for me next week.

What is Greece like today?

When I started on the lesson proper I asked the children what they thought Greece was like today. No problems, they replied, Mano in the class lived there for two years and he can tell us. So we asked him to provide a few select facts:

- they had little statues of people like Hercules
- there were lots of clean beaches and loads of shops
- their writing is different – they have a completely different alphabet
- their numbers are similar.

Brainstorming: What was Ancient Greece like?

So – that is modern Greece. We must now work our way back into Ancient Greece – how long ago was it? Lots of answers and most quite reasonable. I suggested we focused on 2,500 years ago.

Chronology exercise: AD/BC problems!

I explained that now we are AD people – **A**nno **D**omini, the year of Our Lord, counting forward from Christ's birth. The Ancient Greeks, I said firmly, they were BC people, **B**efore **C**hrist. Of course the Greeks didn't know that themselves, but we now count backwards from the birth of Christ. So we would start doing the 500 years backward crawl. The children by now had the idea, but were also convinced that whoever invented this sytem wanted his head testing.

So, once we get 2,500 years back, it is not likely that the Ancient Greeks will be the same as us, or even similar. They will think different thoughts, wear different clothes, behave differently and often look very strange to our modern eyes. We then started to look for clues in the pictures I had brought along.

Using pictures about Ancient Greece

When thinking about this project it was clear to me that we would need pictures, but most of the specifically educational sets I examined were far too expensive and didn't have a broad coverage. So I did an old trick taught me by a respectable colleague: I bought a book on Ancient Greek art and architecture for only £6.95 and cut out the best illustrations – about 35 of them. I then mounted them on A4 card and had them laminated, so that for a minimum expenditure we had a versatile, useful and valuable set of sources that could keep everyone busy.

Working on the pictures

The children worked in pairs with the illustrations, looking for a 'difference from us', and after a couple of minutes they came up to the board to write down their findings while I showed their picture to the rest of the children. This gave me a certain control over the situation, as the first sight of so many nude statues can crack the *sang froid* of the best of children. I lightened the occasion by introducing my own foolish jokes, making me the misbehaver. When about to show the Venus de Milo, for example, I told them they were about to see a picture of a girl who would never pick her nose again.

Noses figured quite a bit – several children found it hard to understand the pictures, and didn't realize that many statues had lost their noses, thinking at first that Ancient Greeks had funny noses. It was important to spend time on this so that the children got the correct view without being made to feel stupid. We talked a little about what might happen when tall statues in the course of time crashed down. What might get damaged first? We noted as well how easy it was to misread pictures, that it was as easy as misreading text.

The list on the board now read: funny beards, hunt lions, ride bareback, used axes not guns: only wore cloaks, no shoes. I quizzed them about what this all might mean, what it could be telling us. They said the Greeks seem to have been a fierce and fit people, quite tough.

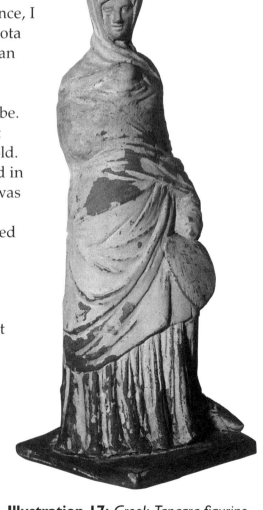

Hunting for evidence

To extend this habit of focusing on meaning and hunting for evidence, I had them look at a Greek terracota Tanagra figurine in a cloak and an oddly balanced sun-hat, and clasping a fan. Was she dressed like this for fashion's sake? Maybe. But the sun-hat and fan suggest she's hot, the cloak that she's cold. Some children thought she lived in a very changeable climate and was prepared for anything, others thought she had a fever. I stressed that our thinking was educated guesswork – we weren't just making silly suggestions.

Questions

Why do some statues have short hair, I asked, are they afraid of nits? The children laughed and said scornfully, no it is hot, so short hair is comfortable. Is that why they sometimes wear so little? Maybe.

Illustration 17: *Greek Tanagra figurine*

What a lot of gods and temples the Ancient Greeks had! I put forward the suggestion that if we get dug up in 2,500 years time they will find the remains of schools, factories and supermarkets. Will they think these were our temples? The children liked this idea. We discussed the nice patterns they had in those days, skilfully done, but dull colours – earth colours.

Classroom atmosphere

I am trying here to give some flavour of the relaxed chatter to and fro between class and teacher as we browsed among the pictures. It needs to move slowly, and as it moves slowly there is time to guide, nudge, give direction to the ideas. At the end I asked the children to write down just three sentences starting with 'My guess about the Ancient Greeks being different from us is...'

Gemma put in a minority report, seeing similarities, not differences.

Here are two examples of what they had to say:
(spelling corrected)

The Greeks were very different to us, as they didn't wear any shoes on their feet, and the women only wore cloth draped over them. Which I suppose was fashionable for their time. They believed in many Greek Gods one of which was Neptune.

The Greeks loved making sculptures of gods, and had sculptures all over their towns and cities. The Greeks also loved to vote and debate about things, even what they were going to have for lunch.

I would not like to have lived in Greece in those times, because the men were so sexist, as they didn't let women vote. Only the free men were allowed to vote, which were men who were not slaves or servants.

Olivia

Why Greeks weren't THAT different to us
6E made a list of all the things they thought the Greeks were different to us but I looked at the list really carefully and half of them weren't different to us.

I think we are very like the Greeks, we might even have inherited some of what they used to do like we're hypocrites, we're clever, some of us are thieves!

The Greeks weren't THAT different. One of the things that is different to us is they loved sculpting and we don't that much.

Gemma

Session 2 What the Ancient Greeks thought about life and death

The lesson started with reviewing the jigsaw puzzle activity, and then moved on to learning about Greek cities and attitudes to life and death.

Learning objectives

The objectives of this session were to learn about the Ancient Greeks from:

- a fragmentary source, the jigsaw puzzle
- a map of the region
- documentary sources, to start exploring Ancient Greek attitudes to life and death.

Resources

The resources used were the jigsaw (Illustration 17), a map of Ancient Greece (Illustration 1), Pindar's Ode and Menander's Ode.

> ### Pindar's Ode
> All of a rush, we have a winner of this race.
> Richly endowed with youth, and now full of hope for
>   the future.
> Though his pocket is empty, his heart lifts up with hope
> As he flies into manhood.
> But this time of pleasure has its term, and soon fate will
>   stop him dead
> How short that season of delight –
> No more than a shadow in a dream.
> Yet when godly splendour is poured out
> And a youth shines like gold –
> How sweet life is!

> ### Menander's Ode
> Think of life as something like a festival
> Or a visit to a strange city, full of noise,
> Buying and selling, thieving, gambling
> And play parks. If you have to leave this place early,
> Well just think you have gone on to find a better hotel.
> You paid your bills, and left no enemies behind.
> Those who hang on get tired, spent up, grow old
> And can't make out what's wrong with themselves.
> They think it's other people's fault,
> And when they finally go, they don't have an easy passage.

The teaching

Solution of the jigsaw puzzle

I was genuinely amazed at how well the children had coped with the jigsaw task. In fact they rather took the wind out of my sails, as I wanted to mock a little at the very idea that tso few pieces could be reconstructed into a logical whole. What had this exercise taught us about doing history? It was a moment for genuine praise and the delight that that could bring to the children.

I asked what they thought the subject of the picture was and received the following replies: *'A party, gods having a fight, ladies dancing, one handing something to another, playing instruments, one looks to me like she is going to slap the other round the face, showing off, selling something, a maid handing jewellery to her mistress.'* I indicated that all the ideas were good, and almost all equally possible.

Archaeological reconstruction

Would they now like to see how the archaeologists had reconstructed the scene and how it was interpreted? They would, and were a bit shaken to find two boys boxing. *'But they look like girls.'* They aren't wearing tops, they could be boys. Well, what are we to say – did the archaeologists get it right or wrong? I had them look closely. There's red at the top and black at the bottom, so that's right. They are wearing jewellery (I hadn't seen this myself, but hastily asserted the rights of boys to wear jewellery and got some odd looks). There's a boxing glove missing – the boxing gloves aren't very convincing. The children rambled on for some time discussing various interpretations until I felt it was the right moment to say, 'What do you think that this exercise has taught us about doing history?'

Class discussion on 'what is history?'

'Often you don't get the answer you expect'. 'Sometimes you are surprised by the past'. 'There are no right or wrong answers. Different people have different interpretations'. 'History's difficult – there are bits missing. You can never be sure. The past comes to us in bits and pieces.' I was so pleased with these responses that I asked them to write a couple of sentences in their notebooks describing what doing history is like. When they had finished we all looked at some painted plaster one pupil, John, had created at home, and discussed the problems of painting wet plaster. Everyone admired his work and even thought that it having cracked in two pieces on the bus to school made it more 'like real'.

How the geography of Greece affected the development of cities

I explained to the children that now we were going to look particularly at Greek towns, especially Athens. We thought first about how a land made up of mountains and valleys that led down to the sea could have promoted cities. The children pulled me up short by asking how the people got there in the first place – I muttered vaguely about invasions from the north and access from the sea, but felt that their question was a good one deserving a fuller answer, had there been time.

So there they were, farming the valleys, worried in case more invaders from the north come over the mountains or in from the sea. What could they do to be safer? The children wisely stated that the best policy was to build a safe place in the middle surrounded by walls, a place to retreat to.

Need for gods

What's another way to ensure success and safety, rain when you want it, sunshine at the right moment? The children yawned ever so slightly and said 'gods'. So there would be some temples inside the walls. I was by now feeling very cross with myself – this was the kind of teaching I really hated, leaking out information, bit by bit.

Greek town government

We struggled on talking about courts and places for discussion. The children actually found the information about the agora interesting, particularly revelling in the idea of voting politicians and generals into exile by ostracism. They thought it would be rather fun to secretly mark a piece of broken pot and so send somebody of importance away for ten years.

Reading documents

I introduced the documents, but noted at once that several children switched off at the sight of 'reading to do', and I was almost apologetic about it. We looked first at Pindar's Ode, and began to get the children to search for their own words and phrases to express its sentiments: *'You can't live for ever; there are bad parts in your life as well as good; he's won this race, but might lose the next; live for the moment, you might be dead tomorrow; enjoy life while you can.'*

The children took down their ideas in their notebooks and then we turned to Menander's Ode. I told them we would use this to check whether we were right in what we were beginning to feel about the Ancient Greek attitude to life and death. Although the children who disliked reading shuddered slightly, I felt that now we had a purpose for reading (to check whether our perceptions were right), it was a slightly better task. The children quickly volunteered their versions: *'Get on with life; don't hang on, enjoy things; move on, don't stay in one place.'* They discussed the moving on, and quickly saw this was about death, and wondered whether it could be an expression of a belief in reincarnation. They continued: *'For older folk life is no longer an adventure; when they die, they don't do so easily; enjoy life while you can; if you die, die happy.'*

Class discussion

The discussion then 'took off' as the children talked about the Greek view of death with great interest and concern. They talked happily, as if released in being able to discuss such a subject easily.

Pupils' poems

Finally they set to work to commit their ideas to paper: Here are two versions of the Pindar Ode:
(Spelling corrected)

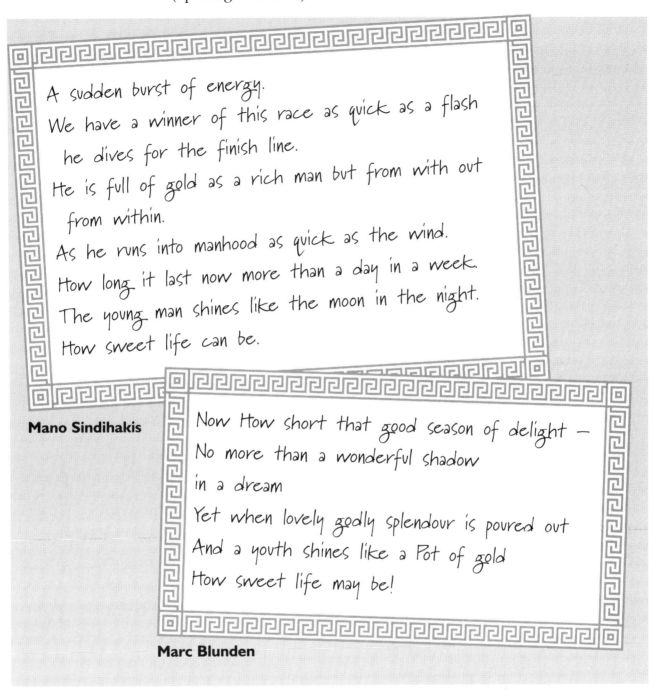

A sudden burst of energy.
We have a winner of this race as quick as a flash
he dives for the finish line.
He is full of gold as a rich man but from with out
from within.
As he runs into manhood as quick as the wind.
How long it last now more than a day in a week.
The young man shines like the moon in the night.
How sweet life can be.

Mano Sindihakis

Now How short that good season of delight —
No more than a wonderful shadow
in a dream
Yet when lovely godly splendour is poured out
And a youth shines like a Pot of gold
How sweet life may be!

Marc Blunden

Session 3 Ancient Greeks' views on democracy

In the next lesson, still not shaken free of my insane desire to instruct, I proposed to induct them into the functioning of democracy, using the famous speech of Pericles.

The speech of Pericles

We love beauty without being vulgar and we honour wisdom without being wimps. We don't boast about our wealth, merely see it as a means to do well. When we are poor we are not ashamed, but try to struggle out of our poverty. Our citizens see their public duties as quite as important as their private life. We see the man who stays away from the debate as useless for we know that we must talk everything out before we act. We do good to others, and so make them our fast friends. Our city is an education for the whole of Greece, we are the most independent, many-sided and self reliant people in hands and brain in the world.

Not everyone was so sure as Pericles. Socrates, a famous philosopher of the time, questioned everything, so that eventually in 399 BC they made him take poison. I also introduced his views on democracy.

Socrates' Views

Imagine a ship where the captain is a big strong man, a good sailor, but a little deaf and short-sighted. All the crew are squabbling as to who should steer the ship, although none have had any training – indeed they laugh at the very idea of expertise. They try to persuade the captain to trust them, and throw over-board anyone else he seems to trust. They make the captain drunk to gain control, and then raid the stores to hold a wild party. They do not see that a genuine captain has to study the seasons of the year, the stars, the winds, nor do they understand the value of long years of experience.

The teaching

Role play activity about Greek ideas of democracy

We set all the furniture aside and made the children sit in a great circle. I explained that the *demos* consisted of the free men of Athens, so who was excluded? They quickly got the idea that there were to be no women or children, but then got stuck. I said 'What about that word *free*?' and they quickly responded, 'Oh yes, no prisoners'. Well yes, but what else? One reckless boy suggested that married men might have been excluded (as 'unfree' in his terminology) but eventually we got to slaves. So, Ancient Greek democracy was a bit exclusive and not quite so nice as we had expected.

Reading documents: Pericles' and Socrates' views on Athenian democracy

I said that one man who really liked democracy was Pericles, and read to them his speech. But when I asked for their responses they were rather hostile '*He's boastful; very upfront; he would give his life for Athens; he's a hypocrite – he says Athenians aren't boastful and that's just what he is; the women and children would have said "leave that lot to get on".*'

Questioning Socrates

So we progressed to the idea that some people didn't like Athenian democracy. We looked at what Socrates had to say. The children thought he was very critical of the *demos*, and so I suggested that they spend a minute or two thinking up questions to ask Socrates (in role as members of the demos). This was done rather too quickly and some children got mixed up between Pericles and Socrates, but by and large they got the idea. They asked 'Where would you find a strong man to rule?' and 'Are you a strong man?' I explained that although I was old, wise and clever, they would really need someone young for the task. I suggested that one of my students, Alcibiades, would be just the man. They asked what I had against Pericles, and why was I not willing to give the free men a chance. I denounced debate and voting, describing them as country clodhoppers full of drink. They grew quite cross at my insults and it is not too surprising that at the end of a vigorous debate, they decided I should take poison.

Children's writing

I asked them quickly to note down why they liked democracy and what was so good about it. Aelfred, who finds writing immensely difficult, preferred to write a lament for Socrates (Spelling corrected):

Socrates died yesterday
Socrates died yesterday
and his last words were
at least I died
for what I did, not
like some of you
at least I died honestly
and for what I did

Aelfred de Sigley

In the next lesson we turned to the last two documents in my collection, representing the ideas of Greek scientists. To tell the truth I was a bit wary of handling this material, fearing that it was just too gnomic and different for children to get a grip on. Some of the children still showed signs of switching off when the documents were produced, and I wondered whatever might happen when we turned to these.

In fact, on the way to school (as so often, at the last minute) I found the answer. We would start where we were, and not approach the hurdle direct. My great teacher, Dorothy Heathcote, always told me, 'Think where you want to start, and then take five steps back'.

Learning objective   The objective for this session was to develop in children an understanding of Greek science.

Resources   We used two documents, commentaries on Anaximander and Heraclitus by John Burnet.

Commentary on Anaximander

And besides this, there was an eternal motion, in which was brought about the origin of the worlds.

He says that something capable of begetting hot and cold out of the eternal was separated off at the original of this world. From this arose a sphere of flame which fitted close round the air surrounding the earth as the bark round a tree. When this had been torn off and shut up in certain rings, the sun, the moon, and stars came into existence.
The earth swings free, held in its place by nothing. It stays where it is because of its equal distance from everything. Its shape is hollow and round, and like a stone pillar.
Living creatures arose from the moist element as it was evaporated by the sun. Man was like another animal, namely a fish, in the beginning.
The first animals were produced in the moisture, each enclosed in a prickly bark. As they advanced in age, they came out upon the drier part. When the bark broke off, they survived for a short time.
Further, he says that originally man was born from animals of another species.
He declares that at first human beings arose in the inside of fishes, and after having been reared like sharks, and become capable of protecting themselves, they were finally cast ashore and took to land.

> **Commentary on Heraclitus**
>
> God is day and night, winter and summer, war and peace, surfeit and hunger; but he takes various shapes, just as fire, when it is mingled with spices, is named according to the savour of each.
>
> It is the opposite which is good for us.
>
> You cannot step twice into the same river; for fresh waters are ever flowing in upon you.
>
> To God all things are fair and good and right, but men hold some things wrong and some right.
>
> We must know that war is common to all and strife is justice, and that all things come into being and pass away through strife.
>
> The way up and the way down is one and the same.
>
> In the circumference of a circle the beginning and end are common.
>
> Men do not know how what is at variance agrees with itself. It is an attunement of opposite tensions, like that of the bow and the lyre.
>
> If you do not expect the unexpected, you will not find it: for it is hard to be sought out and difficult.
>
> Those who seek for gold dig up much earth and find little.
>
> Nature loves to hide.

The teaching

What equipment would we need to construct a science laboratory today?

I began the lesson asking the children what they would need to construct a science laboratory today, writing all they told me on the board: Bunsen burner, goggles, tripod and gauze, beaker, stirring rod, spatula, thermometer, chemicals. I realized they were describing the school laboratory, so said, 'Let's get away from chemistry – is there anything else scientists use?' The answers were: microscope, telescope, binoculars, a project (an experiment to do), magnifying glass. It was interesting that when Rosanne said 'a project' I didn't understand – it took several children to explain. But this time, as usual, was well spent – never drive on, just because you don't understand what a child is saying.

Brainstorming ideas about science projects the Ancient Greeks might have tried to investigate

I next asked the children which of the list on the board the Ancient Greeks would have had to help them when they set out to explain the natural world (which we called, of course, *their* project). And of course we found they had very little. This had taken half an hour, which may seem wasteful, but they had warmed up their brains and established a line of direction. We could now ask the hard question: 'If I were an Ancient Greek, 2,500 years ago, and I hadn't got all that, but I still wanted to explain the natural world, what would my project be?' The children's responses were:

'Why and how does water disappear?
Is illness a punishment from the gods?
Why do we stay on the ground and not float away?
Why are we fixed here?
How does the human body work?

What are rocks and plants for and how do they get here?
How does nature work – what is it?
Why are we here?
What is the meaning of it?
What is higher than the clouds?
*What is the ball of fire in the sky in the daytime, and what are the pin
     pricks of light at night?*
What is beneath our feet?
Why is it hot in some places and cold in others?
What makes it change?
Who invented us?'

These are the children's questions, as they posed them, and if ever
anyone wants to argue about the capacity of children to empathize
with the distant past, I rest my case. These are some of the most
exciting ideas I have had from children in the lifetime of *this* project.

**Reading documents
about Ancient
Greek science**

We looked now at the writing by Anaximander, to check whether
our guesses about the nature of Greek 'projects' had been correct.
Each time he seemed to mention something we had put on the
board we gave it a tick.

I also asked them to consider how well they thought Anaximander
was doing, considering it was 2,500 years ago and he had none of
our modern tools. I even asked the children to mark him out of 10 –
they gave him from 6 to 9, and of course I asked them why they
gave their marks: *'Compared with what we do, with what we have, he does
very well. Remember, he's on his own.' 'He knows more than we do. He is so
close to discovering things it took people thousands more years to find.'* I
asked Peter, who only gave a 6, for his opinion. He said, *'Yes,
Anaximander is very good, but he doesn't test his ideas – that's the real
difference between now and then.'*

Having coped spectacularly well with Anaximander, we had a go at
someone much harder – Heraclitus. They were now pelting me with
ideas (the leaders, like Mano, with a lot, but many of the others, too):
'God is everywhere; you have to learn things the hard way'.
'Nothing is the same again.'
*'God feels everything is right – bad as well as good, because God can forgive
 and man can't.'*
*'Evil is ever present, going up is hard, down easy, but the path is the
 same one.'*
'The world is a circle, everything keeps going round.'
'Things you expect to be opposite are often the same.'
'If you dig for gold you won't find much.'
'Good things hide, like animals in a forest.'

When asked for marks for Heraclitus, most people said 7-8, but
Stephen only gave 4, saying his ideas were good, but he never
develops them. I felt pleased and proud when this lesson ended and
reflected how often it was that lessons that began with anxiety
ended in delight. Maybe I have been reading too much Heraclitus.